D1271270

FULLY ALIVE!

**YOUR PERSONAL JOURNEY INTO
DISCOVERING HIDDEN MYSTERIES**

JOHN PAUL JACKSON

Streams
TM   MINISTRIES PUBLISHING

FULLY ALIVE!
Your Personal Journey Into Discovering Hidden Mysteries
By John Paul Jackson

Published by Streams Publishing House
www.streamsministries.com
1-888-441-8080

Unless otherwise noted, Scripture quotations are taken from
the New King James Version. Copyright 1979, 1980, 1982 by Thomas
Nelson, Inc.

Scripture quotations marked (AMP) are taken from the
Amplified Bible, Copyright © 1954, 1958, 1962, 1964, 1965, 1987 by
The Lockman Foundation. Used by permission.

Scripture quotations marked (NLT) are taken from the Holy
Bible, New Living Translation, copyright © 1996, 2004, 2007 by
Tyndale House Foundation. Used by permission of Tyndale
House Publishers, Inc., Carol Stream, Illinois 60188. All rights
reserved.

Scripture quotations marked (NIV) are taken from the Holy
Bible, New International Version®, NIV®. Copyright © 1973, 1978,
1984, 2011 by Biblica, Inc.™ Used by permission of Zondervan. All
rights reserved worldwide. www.zondervan.com The "NIV" and
"New International Version" are trademarks registered in the
United States Patent and Trademark Office by Biblica, Inc.™

This book incorporates content from John Paul Jackson's
television series "Dreams and Mysteries" and other sources.

ISBN: 978-0-9858638-8-3
Printed in the United States of America

FOR MORE INFORMATION:
USA: www.streamsministries.com
Canada: www.streamscanada.com
1-888-441-8080

DEDICATION

*To dreamers who want to explore
and for explorers who seek answers
to mysteries.*

CONTENTS

CHAPTER 1

THE MYSTERY OF DESTINY

The chance encounter at a coffee shop leads to a new job. A late bus reunites you with an old friend. A missed appointment spares you from being involved in an accident. Chance? Fluke? Coincidence?

Is a coincidence really a serendipity, a déjà vu, or some cosmic, random selection? How strange does a situation have to get in order for us to call it a "coincidence"?

How many of us miss "coincidences" by mere seconds because we're just not in the right place at the right time? Perhaps we were just moments early—or moments late.

Can a single coincidence change your life and destiny?

Perhaps you live a life full of "coincidences." Maybe you have seasons when the story line of your life could not have been written better by the best Hollywood screenwriter. Then, in other seasons, nothing.

The road to destiny is littered with coincidences. Destiny isn't the same as "fate." It's not rigid. It's not fixed. It's not predetermined. Destiny has twists and turns. Coincidences are the milestones God uses to tell us we are on the right track.

Destiny is not always a straight line. Destiny is more like a tapestry that is woven every day by the decisions we make. God is the One who gives us our destiny. God gives it, but we get to walk it out. This is what makes it a mystery—the mystery of destiny.

A mysterious tension takes place between the choices we make and what is known as "destiny." What is destiny, anyway? Is destiny the same as fate? Is it fate that you're reading this book, or is it part of God's master plan? Can a destiny be lost? What happens to the destiny of those who die prematurely? What happens to the destiny of those who simply choose another path?

Can a person miss their destiny? If God truly knows the end from the beginning and the beginning from the end, then wouldn't God know that you would choose a different path? Does God waste a perfectly good destiny on a person who had no intentions of using it in the first place?

What if God's destiny for you worked like a navigation device? What if He has a set of directions that will take you exactly where He wants you? Would one wrong turn make you become lost for years or, instead of giving up on you when you make the wrong choice, could God just recalculate? God has chosen a destiny for you. He isn't going to take it back just because you make a few bad choices. We have all made bad choices. We are grateful that God has given us grace.

An oft-quoted verse of Scripture states, "The gifts and the calling of God are irrevocable" (Romans 11:29). This means that when God gives us gifts, talents or abilities, He is not going to take them back. We have an eye color and a physical stature that was predetermined we would have. We can't change it. In the same way, God has given us gifts at birth and they stay with us for life, even if we don't use them!

All of us wonder about our destiny. How does God let us know what our destiny is? The answer is simple: He calls us.

God calls us into our destiny in many ways. One of the ways He calls us is by supernatural means, in ways that are beyond natural or without a normal explanation.

One amazing way God can call a person is to give them an encounter with God where He shows the person their whole life unfolding right before their very eyes. It is like watching a movie on fast-forward. He could show us everyone we are destined to influence and impact. He can show us the whole picture in one experience, one vision, one dream, but usually it doesn't happen that way, and it's a good thing, too.

GOD HAS GIVEN US GIFTS AT BIRTH AND THEY STAY WITH US FOR LIFE, EVEN IF WE DON'T USE THEM!

Just imagine if a navigation device gave us all the directions to our destination at once and then shut off. Would your memory recall it? Mine wouldn't! That wouldn't be fair to us. We would get rid of that device and get another one real fast.

Just like a navigation device, God gives us directions as we go along our way. Our responsibility is to leave the driveway first. We have to be willing to get out of any ruts we may be in. We have to exercise faith. Once we are in motion, God will give us directions.

One of the ways that God helps us to reach our destination is through a "prophetic word." A prophetic word is simply the heart of God revealed to one person for the benefit of someone else. Why would God trust another human being with something as important as our very own destiny? Well, a prophetic word isn't actually our destiny, but more like a street sign intended to help us reach our destiny.

A prophetic word is like a sign. One road sign might be "Caution" and another "Yield" or yet another "Do Not Enter." Like all signs, the sign itself isn't the destination. The sign is simply there to help us reach our destination.

This sign could be a warning of something coming up on the road ahead. Maybe it is something like, "Next Rest Stop 5 Miles." Such a sign would be a big help if we thought we were in a sprint but actually were running a marathon. The sign can help us reach our destination by providing direction, encouragement, or even warning.

> A "PROPHETIC WORD" IS SIMPLY THE HEART OF GOD REVEALED TO ONE PERSON FOR THE BENEFIT OF SOMEONE ELSE. IT IS NOT OUR DESTINY, BUT MORE LIKE A STREET SIGN INTENDED TO HELP US REACH OUR DESTINY.

Not every prophetic word is a "thus saith the Lord" proclamation to the nation. When we allow ourselves to believe that the "prophetic word" has only this one narrow purpose, we miss out on an important way that God speaks to His people.

Consider that one of the first prophetic words Jesus gave during His ministry was not a proclamation to the nation of Israel. The first recorded prophetic word of Jesus was for one person: Nathaniel. When Jesus saw Nathaniel approaching He said, "Behold, an Israelite indeed, in whom is no deceit" (John 1:47).

Why did Jesus say that? Personal prophecy can sometimes seem unusual and a little out in left field, but to the person receiving a very real "word" from God, it is the right message at just the right time. Nathaniel found out what God thought about him, and that must have been just what he needed to answer the call of Christ.

Sometimes we think we know what God has told us, but opposition comes and we question if God has a purpose and plan for our lives at all. Sometimes we need a reminder. Sometimes we need a sign.

Are you looking for a sign? A good place to start is by reading the Bible. It's full of them. The Bible sensitizes you to any other sign that God might want to use to help you reach your destiny.

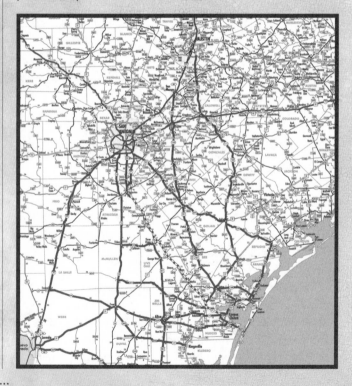

Not all signs and directions from God are crystal clear. Having crystal-clear directions is not always a good thing because of something I call the "Clarity-Cost Principle."

Think about how we receive and follow directions to a geographic location. Following directions to a new address can sometimes be confusing. Ask anyone who has ever been lost while trying to follow the directions generated by their cell phone.

Have you ever been given directions somewhere and nothing seemed to look like what was described? Let's say the directions tell us to drive about five miles and look for a large red barn, but after driving eight miles we haven't seen a barn. In that instant, we will generally do one of three things.

We may wonder if we missed the barn, or a sign or landmark that would tell us it's time to make the next decision. When we become concerned enough, we may make a U-turn. Making a U-turn would be the best decision if we were really going in the wrong direction, but if we are going in the right direction and make a U-turn, it just delays our arrival.

Or we may begin to question the directions themselves. We start to wonder if the directions really meant a red barn or if it really meant a red storage shed.

Or we may simply settle back and trust the directions. We may trust our ability to decipher the signs even when the signs don't come at the time we expect them.

How often do we make a decision to give up, only to find that the landmark was just over the next hill? In the same way, staying on the path God has planned for us is not a precise walk, and neither are His directions. This is something we are wise to consider when wondering when God is going to give us direction.

The Clarity-Cost Principle is a spiritual principle that states simply this: The clearer the direction we receive from God, the greater the cost or difficulty it will be to fulfill what He has called us to do.

THE CLARITY-COST PRINCIPLE states that the clearer the direction we receive from God, the more difficult it will be to fulfill it.

Clarity is given mostly for directions that will cost us dearly. It is given clearly, so that during the most difficult times, which are bound to come, we still cannot forget that it was God who told us to do it.

Noah is a great example of this. Decades ago, a young Bill Cosby burst out as a brand-new comic with a routine about God talking to Noah. In it, God said, "Noah, I want you to build an ark!" Noah responded, "Right! (pause) What's an ark?" You could just hear the gulp in Noah's voice wondering how much this was going to cost, how long it was going to take, and what on earth it was for, since it had never rained on earth before and he didn't live anywhere near an ocean.

Let's put this in modern times and say that a young man named Jordan is called to be a leader of young adults. Jordan may have received that call in a variety of ways. He may have a desire in his heart to lead young adults, and that would be one level of calling. That would make it a "desire call."

Let's say, however, that Jordan hears an audible voice of God telling him that he is called to lead young adults. That call is a lot different. That call is very clear. He would likely never forget the day and hour and the exact place where he was when he heard it.

Now let's go further and say that Jordan has a name for his destiny: "Inner City Youth Leader." He knows that his destiny is to gather and lead an inner-city group of young adults that will change their neighborhood through community service. That's the destiny that God has gifted and called him to.

Imagine Jordan now wrapping a giant spiritual rope around his waist in order to fulfill the purpose for which God created him. At one end of the rope is Jordan, at the other is God. The rope itself can be very long, or it can be very short.

If Jordan has not been given a clear message from God as to how or where he's supposed to fulfill his destiny, it doesn't mean God doesn't have a plan for him. It just means that in God's plans for Jordan, at this point anyway, the rope is long. Jordan has a great deal of flexibility in how he carries out the plan. Some people call this "great grace." Jordan right now can do a lot of things without violating what God has told him to do.

Now let's say that Jordan is getting along great with the young adults. They seem to like him and want to hang out with him. Jordan still has a lot of slack in his rope, but what if God intervenes in what Jordan is doing and gives him a clearer direction to his destiny?

Let's say that Jordan gets clear direction to leave New York and move to Chicago. Suddenly, Jordan doesn't have a lot of choice. He has to go in that direction or miss his destiny. The rope just got shorter with less flexibility. It starts with a prophetic word from someone. That same night, Jordan has a dream where he's helping people in a poor neighborhood clean up their streets. The next day, a third coincidence happens and he gets an email from a friend inviting him to a youth event in Chicago.

With each sign that coincides with another, the call gets a little clearer. Before the three signs came, Jordan was on a very long leash, but now the roadmap to his destiny in God came into clearer focus.

Because of the Clarity-Cost Principle, with greater clarity comes greater cost. When we have clarity, we don't have room for flexibility. What does that clarity cost us? It costs us our choices. The clearer the direction from God, the less room we have to deviate from those directions.

Let me provide another example. Let's just say that God tells me to move to Texas. Texas is a big state. I could move anywhere in Texas and I would still be following the perfect will of God for my life, up to that point. However, if God tells me to move to the Dallas area, I no longer have the grace to move to Houston. I have to live in the Dallas area, and if God tells me to move to a specific suburb of Dallas, I no longer have the flexibility to live outside of that suburb.

It costs us something with each degree of clarity we receive in revelation from God about our future. Many times the clarity of the call means that what we used to get away with, we can no longer get away with. What we used to be able to do, we are no longer able to do.

MANY TIMES THE CLARITY OF THE CALL MEANS THAT WHAT WE USED TO GET AWAY WITH, WE CAN NO LONGER GET AWAY WITH. WHAT WE USED TO BE ABLE TO DO, WE ARE NO LONGER ABLE TO DO.

Whether or not I reach my destiny is up to me. I can untie that spiritual rope at any time. I can "un-volunteer." But what choice could I possibly make that would lead to greater joy than fulfilling the very purpose for which I was created?

The mystery of destiny is this: On one side of the spiritual connection, we have an incredible God who is perfect. He made each of us unlike anyone else on earth. Even before He created us, He had a plan that would utilize our gifts and talents to the utmost.

God caused both you and me to be birthed at this precise time in history. This is a time like no other, because it is the time when our plan is most needed in the earth. God placed each of us in the very city on earth where we could fulfill that plan.

What choice could I possibly make that would lead to greater joy than fulfilling the very purpose for which I was created?

At that end of the connection, the spiritual rope where God is, sits God's destiny for our lives. On the other end of the rope is just a human being—me, you, others. Each of us is a bundle of faults, fears and sin. We're lonely souls who need to hold fast to the rope to stay tethered to God. We hold tight to that spiritual rope, and there's one thing we can be sure of—God never lets go of His end.

THE WONDERFUL THING ABOUT DREAMS...

...is that, when we understand them, they reveal facets of our destiny. It could be as subtle as a simple course correction, or it can be a complete picture of our future, full of vibrant color and supernatural splendor. Think about the dream that Joseph had about the stars and the sheaves of wheat. That was quite a dream!

Dreams are messages from eternity. When we interpret their meaning, we can catch a glimpse of the future and our place in it.

The dreamer is in a large room with lots of people. She can see that someone is on stage speaking, so she starts looking around for a seat. She sees an usher and apologizes for being late. She doesn't know why she was late, she just knew that everybody else was already seated and the speaker had already started.

The usher said, "Kim," but the dreamer doesn't know how he knew her name. He said, "Kim, you're not late. You don't speak until after he's finished."

The dreamer said, "What? I'm not speaking."

The usher just laughed and said, "You always say that."

He then led the dreamer to the front row. At this point, she was starting to freak out. She didn't know what to say. She didn't have any notes. She was not prepared.

The next thing she knows, she's up on stage talking, and everybody seems to be enjoying it. She's not nervous, she doesn't want it to end, but then she looks down and she's not fully dressed. She can't believe it. This whole time she's been up on stage, and she doesn't have on all her clothes. She doesn't think anyone noticed. As she finishes up her speech, she tries to hide behind the microphone stand. Then she wakes up.

This is a "calling dream." It has several key points to it that will help the dreamer reach her destiny.

First of all, this dream is calling her to a public role, or to a role where she'll have influence over large groups of people. She may not recognize that calling yet, as evidenced in the dream by her thinking she was just supposed to be part of the audience, but God has created within her the ability to influence others. He's given her what the Bible calls "favor with man."

God wants her to start preparing now to be ready when He gives her the platform to speak to large groups of people. Part of that preparation might be overcoming a fear of speaking in public.

Another part that is emphasized in this dream is that in order for the dreamer to come across as credible and believable, for her to reach the audience she's supposed to reach, she needs to be transparent.

Nakedness in dreams usually represents an ability, or inability, to be open and transparent. She's uncovering herself in the dream for the purpose of gaining trust with her audience. In essence, the transparency is that she believes it is more important that someone connect with her at a human level than it is for her to look like she has all the answers.

Transparency is big to God. Yes, of course He wants us to learn from our mistakes, but He also wants us to share what we learned through those mistakes with others. This is again because destiny isn't always a straight line.

For some of us, it is a series of twists and turns. We often think we've missed it. We make a wrong turn, we feel that we've missed our window of opportunity to follow God, but you know what? We haven't. God is always right there with us, and even when we mess up, to Him it's simple, as simple as...recalculating. ■

Calling dreams come in all shapes and sizes. Calling dreams are when God is telling us where He wants to take us. They can act like a magnifying glass and reveal one small area of our lives that needs some work.

This would be like the dreamer who was destined to a public role but needed to overcome her fear of speaking in public. It could even be the issue of God telling her that when she reaches that point of speaking in front of large groups of people she has to remember to be open and transparent in her messages.

Dreams can also give us the big picture. Dreams can look far, far away into life and show us the big picture, the galactic picture, God's master plan.

That happened for our dreamer when she saw herself up on stage in front of hundreds of people delivering a speech. She felt fearless, transparent, because she had dealt with those issues long ago.

Dreams are a powerful way that God speaks to us about our destiny. They may not be the strangest way, though. Sometimes God will call us into our destiny by a supernatural event that defies explanation.

I call these a "power encounter." I have had several of these powerful yet unusual events happen to me. One occurred just before I went into the ministry.

At the time, my wife and I owned a daycare center with about 100 children in it. Besides that, I was in the corporate business world. I would sometimes help her with the children either before or after I went to work. On one particular day, I had laryngitis. I couldn't even whisper, so there was nothing I could do at the office. I decided I would just stay home. Because the daycare center opened early, Diane would leave generally at about 5:30 in the morning.

After she left, I was lying in bed, but I woke up because there was a light in the room. I thought maybe Diane had left the light on. As I opened my eyes, I realized the light wasn't from the light bulb in the ceiling. A bright light was coming from somewhere else in the room. As soon as I focused on the light, it expanded. It grew so bright that it filled the room, and everything else disappeared from view. There was no furniture or even walls—nothing except brilliant, bright light.

I suddenly was aware that I was in the presence of incredible holiness. It was so incredible that I couldn't stay in the bed. I didn't dare stand up, but instead rolled out of the bed, because it felt just too high. I rolled onto the floor. If I could have got underneath the floor, I would have.

As I rolled from the bed onto the floor, an incredible voice filled the room and reviewed my life for me. The words began telling from when my mother was pregnant with me right up into the present, and right on into the future. In fact, some of the things I heard are things I am doing today.

That supernatural experience, that "power encounter" changed my entire life. In one moment, it literally obliterated the road that I thought I was traveling on.

Experiences like that will mark a person. We never forget them. They can change our course of direction instantly. Why does God communicate with us this way? On the one hand, we can become stubborn and set in our ways. We can become like Saul of Tarsus and independent, but some of us might be like him and need a blinding light on the Damascus road to propel us into our destiny.

The truth is that God created us and so He knows exactly what it's going to take to get our attention. Some people just need a tap on the back. Others need a bright and shining light. But again, before you start asking for a bright, shining light, remember the Clarity-Cost Principle. The greater clarity we receive from God about our destiny, the shorter the leash we will get, and the greater it will cost.

This cost is what Jesus refers to when He tells us to pick up our cross. When we are asked to pick up our own cross, it usually means we're going to have to set something else down—usually what we wanted to do—in order to carry that destiny.

Sometimes, we may not be ready to set it down. Paul received great clarity about what God was asking him to do, but it also came with great persecution. And if that weren't enough, it also came with a thorn in his flesh.

This is all part of the mystery of divine destiny. God knows clearly, but He's not always telling clearly, at least not when we want Him to, and not all at once. Sometimes, that's a good thing.

God's ability to design and create is so vast that no two snowflakes are identical. If God puts that kind of interest into something that falls to the ground and melts in seconds, how much more would He put into our destiny?

No two snowflakes are identical. If God puts that kind of interest into something that falls to the ground and melts in seconds, how much more would He put into our destiny?]

It is nothing to God to give us a dream, a vision, a power encounter or even to speak to us through a prophetic word. God can visit us through an experience that has no earthly explanation.

You might be getting the idea that you were created for greatness. Regardless of how you feel, I know from studying scripture that you were created so precisely that no other person on earth can do what you're called to do. You were birthed here on the earth at the very moment in history—the precise moment—when your gifts and attributes would be needed most.

Just because God's plan for you was created perfect, it doesn't require you to be.

And you were placed in the exact geographical place where you could have the greatest impact on those around you. That's how important you are to God.

Just because God's plan for you was created perfect, it doesn't require you to be. God knew what He was getting when He called you, and His Word says He'll never take back the blueprints He's created for your life. He just... recalculates.

Reflections and Meditations

What kinds of coincidences have you had in your life? Have you found that any of them put you on the right track somewhere?

Have you ever had a dream where you were not fully clothed? What could God have been saying to you?

What do you think about when you hear that a clearer call means a greater cost? Are you prepared to pay that cost to receive that call?

What mistakes has God forgiven you for in your past? As He has recalibrated to lead you into your destiny, are you closer to finally achieving it than you ever have been before?

What specific steps could you take today to draw closer to Him?

CHAPTER 2

THE MYSTERY OF TIME

You and I have a love-hate relationship with time. We never seem to have enough of it. We treat it like a commodity. We try to buy more of it. We search out ways to manage time or save time, but do we really have any control over time?

We often wish that we could travel back into time and fix our mistakes, or dream about being able to travel into the future so that we can see the obstacles and bumps in the road ahead. But is time travel possible? Is there a way for us actually to move through time?

Almost all of time exists in two places—the past or the future. Most of our thought life takes place in these two places. Most of us spend too much time thinking about the past, even though we can't change it. How often do we think about our future? Probably not as much as we should. After all, we do have some control of the future, based on decisions we make today.

What about God? Where does He fit into time, or does He? Could it be that God is walking alongside us, experiencing life with us as it's happening, or does God exist outside of time and simply enters in and out of it as He pleases, or is it even more mysterious than that? Could time exist inside of God? That would make the issue of time travel even more interesting, as if it wasn't interesting enough already.

People often wake up to an alarm clock. We leave the house at a certain time to be at work. We watch the clock to know when it is time to eat, when it is time to go home. We lament waiting in traffic, because it costs us time. We get stressed when we're running late somewhere. We're aggravated when we get there, only to have to wait. That was all time we could have spent doing something else. We complain and say, "It's just hurry up and wait!"

Time is more than just something to be controlled. Time is also beautiful. Time is what turns a caterpillar into a butterfly, seeds into flowers, cells into a baby. Time is what gives beat to a melody, so that we can all sing the same song. We have different tools for measuring time—clocks, calendars, birthdays, seasons.

The rate of time is constant, but it doesn't always seem that way. Ask a child and they'll tell you. For them, the day before Christmas or the trip to Disney has to be at least twice as long as the actual day. Ask any husband or wife, and they'll tell you that time can either speed up or slow down depending on who is holding the remote control.

These are ways we perceive time, but does any of this help us to understand it?

To unlock the mystery of time, we have to separate ourselves from it. We have to look at time not just as a reality, but as something that was created. God created time. Time is a created thing. Just as with light, distance, and gravity, time began at Creation.

The book of Genesis starts, "In the beginning God created the heavens and the earth" (Genesis 1:1). At least that is the translation we usually read. The same passage from the Hebrew version of the Torah states, "In the beginning of God's creating." What a beautiful way of describing how everything that was created got created.

When we hear, "In the beginning, God created..." it doesn't tell the whole story. That was really just the beginning of the heavens and earth. It wasn't the beginning of everything. There was something going on before that. For one thing, God existed. No telling what He was doing, but everything we know began when God started creating.

Time began on Day One when God created the heavens and earth. As soon as the heavens and earth were created, there became a past. What was the past? The past was the time before the heavens and earth. Before Heaven and earth is the past. After Heaven and earth is the present. Simple enough, but then it gets interesting.

Time began on Day One when God started creating things. As soon as something is created, there becomes a past, because there is a time before it was created and a time after it was created.

On Day Two, God created the atmosphere and sky, the seas and the land. On Day Three, God created vegetation and seed-bearing plants.

Then we arrive at Day Four. This is when time gets a much-needed boost. God creates the light in the firmament to be used for signs and seasons and days and years. This important development provided a way to measure time.

Time had existed since Day One, but there was no system for measuring it until Day Four. God created a light in the firmament of the heavens. It gave light to the earth, and it could also be used for signs and seasons, days and years. The light measures time as it passes.

How do we know that the sun was created to measure

time? We know because trees and plants were created on Day Three. In our present world, we know that trees need sunlight to grow, so how did they grow before sunlight was created? God is light, and He was all they needed.

God followed a logical process during these six days of creating. He created dry land before creating man. That was so man and other creatures would have a place to live and not drown. From the order of Creation, we can also see that God created a way of measuring time for us. Trees and plants didn't need it. Humans did. Time was created on Day One. God created a way to measure how time passed on Day Four.

God knew that man needed night and day, man needed to know when to work and when to rest. God rested. Man would need to rest, too. The setting sun forced man to stop. What was he busy doing? From the start, man's job description was to subdue the earth, to rule over it, to name what he found in it and codify the names and functions so he could understand it. Only the setting sun stopped him from being carried away with this work.

Time went through another major transition after Day Four. When Adam and Eve fell to temptation in the Garden of Eden and ate from the Tree of the Knowledge of Good and Evil, it caused a series of spiritual and physical dominoes to fall.

Mankind made two enemies on the day sin entered the world. One was the serpent. The other was time. From that moment forward, time began to have a negative effect on man. God had warned Adam that the day he ate from the Tree of Knowledge he would surely die.

> Mankind made two enemies on the day sin entered the world.
>
> 1. The serpent.
> 2. Time.

Before sin entered the Garden, time had a limited role in the lives of Adam and Eve. It told them when it was time to get up and start subduing the earth again. It told them when God would come and walk with them in the cool of the day.

It told them when to go to sleep. Time was filled with subtle, gentle reminders. Time was their friend, a useful tool. After sin, however, time became a constant reminder of man's mortality. That's when the clock started ticking. Adam and Eve grew older. When sin came into the picture, the passing of time got personal because it involved aging and sickness. Time didn't cause them to age. Sin caused them to age. Time just recorded it.

How long do you think Adam and Eve lived before the fateful day when they succumbed to temptation? We have no idea, but we do know how long Adam lived after aging set in due to the Fall. He lived 930 years, just 70 years shy of his 1,000-year birthday. The author of the Psalms wrote that, to God, a day is as a thousand years is to man. Adam died 70 years short of that symbolic number.

Before sin, there was no aging. The fundamental property of sin is that it deteriorates whatever it comes into contact with—people, animals, plants, rocks. All of Creation was affected by sin. It all deteriorates now over time.

Sin caused other ways in which time became our enemy. The past also became a potential enemy. The Tree of the Knowledge of Good and Evil is the ability to know what is good and what is evil. Eating of the tree did not just open the door for the ability to sin. Eating the tree also created the awareness of our sin. The "original sin" became a past-tense action that brought up a new emotion—regret. Everything that came with it—self-condemnation, second-guessing, hindsight—ushered in a new way of viewing the world.

Before Adam and Eve sinned in the Garden, they had no knowledge of good and evil. After they sinned, they remembered the past differently. They remembered the good and the bad. Being able to recall the bad memories that were filled with sin created even more ways to sin—unforgiveness, bitterness, repeating past mistakes.

Most scientists would add to a discussion about time the mystery of the fourth dimension, the space-time continuum. It's fascinating to explore this in the natural realm, but it won't answer spiritual questions.

Thinking about time causes us to wonder about issues such as fate, or if there is an eternal purpose. Does God know our future? How could He know our future when it might depend on the sum of a billion little choices that we haven't even made yet? If God doesn't know our future, how can we trust that He will keep us safe when He doesn't even know what might be around the next corner?

These are the great mysteries of God and time. The answers will help to determine whether we pray in faith or pray in hope. Hope is a wonderful thing, but praying in hope is like bringing a knife to a gunfight. The knife-wielding villain in the Indiana Jones movie had a big, showy knife, but Indiana Jones' gun silenced the knife. We want hope. Hope is powerful. Jesus gives us "blessed hope," yet when we pray, we want to pray in faith.

The fact is, God isn't with us in time. Time exists within God. It is not as if God were outside of time and periodically just entered time when He needed to intervene in our lives. God is always in the past, the present and the future, all at the same "time." How can we be so sure of this fact, this answer to a great mystery?

For one thing, Jesus Himself told us. In three different accounts of the Gospels, Jesus quotes from Exodus 3:6 and tells the Sadducees, "I am the God of Abraham, and the God of Isaac and the God of Jacob." Then Jesus said, "He is not God of the dead, but the living" (Matthew 22:32, Mark 12:26-27, Luke 20:37-38).

Since Abraham, Isaac and Jacob really were dead by the time Jesus walked the earth, what could Jesus have been talking about? He was talking about the majesty of God. God is eternally present with Abraham, Isaac and Jacob. At the same time, He is listening to His Son Jesus teach the Sadducees. At the same time, He is watching me write this book, and at the same time He is watching my great-grandson take his first steps. All of it occurs at the same time.

You can trust God with your life.

You can ask God to forgive your past mistakes.

You can pray in faith for God to guide your future.

What is the result of this answer to an eternal mystery? Here it is: You can trust God with your life. You can ask God to forgive your past mistakes. You can pray in faith for God to guide your future. He is watching your past and your future play out at the very moment you pray. The God who created you is at the other end when you pray.

Pray in faith, knowing that God is never caught by surprise. He has a plan for you. You have a purpose. God designed that plan and your purpose with the full knowledge of what lies around the very next corner.

WHEN WE DREAM, WE ARE FREE OF TIME.

In a sense, it is as if we time travel. I admit this is a funny thought, but I say it because I look at dreams as a dimension of their own.

Dreams are not limited by time or space, logic or reasoning. They exist in their own world. Time works differently in a dream. How often have you had a dream about your past and seen someone you used to know? Maybe they are even dead now, but in your dream they are very much alive and haven't aged a bit.

Perhaps you have a dream that takes place in a house you lived in as a child. That house could have been torn down years ago. At the very least, the trees around it are taller and the streets around it have changed, but there you are, walking around, just as you did years before.

What about dreams where you're back in school? You could be sitting in a classroom surrounded by teenagers, but no one seems to notice that you're old enough to be their parent. Dreams display the eternal nature of God by showing us scenes unencumbered by the limits of time.

The dreamer was back in high school, and he suddenly realizes they are about to take a test. He can't believe it. He doesn't even know what the test is about. So he's rifling through his backpack, trying to look for a book or something so he can find out what class he's in. The only thing he finds in the backpack is a change of clothes and his lunch. No books. Then the dreamer realizes he needs a pencil because the test is on a Scantron form, but all he has is a pen. He is asking everyone around him for a pencil, but they all ignore him. They already started taking the test. Then the guy next to the dreamer starts whispering to him. He's not telling the dreamer the answers on the test, but he's telling the dreamer how he should take the test. All the dreamer can see are the guy's feet. It's as if the dreamer can't look up any higher. He remembers thinking, that's good advice, but what I really could use are the answers. This wasn't the first time the dreamer had a dream that he was back in high school.

Dreams where we are back in school are very common. Sometimes going back in time in a dream is a way God uses to speak to us about an issue that happened during that period of time, but that's not really the case here. The age of the dreamer is not a major factor in the dream. A backpack often represents something that contains our gifts and talents in a positive context, or our burdens in a negative context, but this wasn't the purpose, either. The dream is more about where he is. He is in school taking a test that he's not prepared for.

If I were to give this dream a title, I might call it "Back in school taking a test." That's all we really need to know in order to interpret this dream. This dream is about the dreamer having to go through a period where things he should have learned already were not learned. He is about to get the opportunity to learn those lessons again. Here is why God gave him the dream. God wants him to know that he is still not prepared. The dreamer doesn't know the test is coming. He didn't study. He didn't even know what the test was about. He didn't have a pencil.

This is a warning dream that a test is coming that the dreamer needs to prepare for or else he won't pass it, but there is a source of hope here, and that is the person he couldn't see. The person whose feet he could see is offering him encouragement. He may not be offering what the dreamer thinks he needs, but he is offering what the dreamer probably does need.

Other people in dreams often represent help from Heaven. It could be Jesus, God, or an angel. What is important for the dreamer to know is that God is with them during this test. When no one else around him offers a hand, God will.

This is a common kind of dream. Many people dream about taking a test they aren't prepared for. To understand dreams like this, and to see if we are going around the same mountain over and over again, as the Israelites did in the wilderness, take a look at the scenery. Has the scenery changed, or does it look the same? When we have the same issues in life happening over and over again, there is a good chance that God is letting us retake some tests that we didn't pass the first time.

The popular saying is that God loves us right where we are, but He loves us too much to leave us there. Sometimes He will use a dream to show us that it's time for a change of scenery, to get past a test and move on. ■

Too often we get God and time confused. A popular poem, "Footprints in the Sand," tells about Jesus' footprints appearing on the beach beside our own. During the low periods of our lives, there is only one set of footprints. The poem says it is because those were the times when Jesus carried us.

The sentiment of the poem has made it wildly popular for decades. It makes sense that as we move slowly toward the future, Jesus is right there with us, but here is where the metaphor falls apart. We cannot take the meaning to be that Jesus is discovering new things along the beach during this walk through time with us.

God has never lost knowledge or gained knowledge. It is impossible for God to be somewhere He's never been before. God has already been to the future to satisfy the characteristics of His deity. It is comforting to picture our personal walk with God by the words of this poem, just as it was no doubt comfortable for Adam and Eve to take walks with God in the cool of the day, even before sin entered the world.

As we go through life, God is with us. We have no doubt of this, but He is also back there in the eternal past watching our birth. At the same time, He is in the eternal future watching our offspring, perhaps several generations away, getting married, all at the same time.

Why is this an important mystery to understand? For one thing, when we fully grasp what the eternality of God means, we will never doubt the possibility that He can give us a dream about our future. We will not doubt when He speaks to us through His Word as we have our regular daily devotions. We won't question that a prophetic word could provide a glimpse into events that have not yet happened. Understanding this mystery also helps us visualize how big God is. It expands our appreciation for His majesty.

Most people have had something take place in their lives that didn't make logical sense. It defied statistical probability. They called it a bizarre coincidence, or a divine encounter, or they sought a seer or occultist to interpret it for them. Really, it's the hand of God. Because God created time, He can orchestrate a billion different overlapping and intersecting occurrences at the same time. This is possible with a God who is outside of time.

Looking at time in light of God being outside of it can also help explain parts of the Bible that we might otherwise overlook. Let's apply our new understanding of time to one of the strangest accounts in the Bible: The Mount of Transfiguration (Matthew 17). In this account, Jesus was standing on the Mount with Moses and Elijah, all three of whom are very much alive. The disciples who witnessed it were so taken aback that all they could think to say or do was to pledge to build a building there to remember it.

Sometimes I've been asked, "Is time travel literally possible?" I answer, "Absolutely!" But time travel is not going to happen through some contraption built by man. It will happen, and has happened, through the sovereign will of God.

For example, the Bible cites a mysterious thing called "the great cloud of witnesses." The writer of Hebrews referred to all of the great men and women of faith throughout the Bible as this "cloud" (Hebrews 12:1). The writer, probably Paul, suggests that he and the rest of the early Christians were surrounded by these heroes of the faith and should use that as motivation to finish strong.

One time I was meditating on this verse of Scripture and felt God impress on my heart the fact that He never does anything without a witness. The Biblical requirement of a witness is the very reason why the testimony of witnesses is required in courts of law today. We "witness" to people on the streets about Christ, and we give "testimony" in small groups about what God is doing in our lives. These things are common to us, but what is this cloud of witnesses?

> "THEREFORE WE ALSO, SINCE WE ARE SURROUNDED BY SO GREAT A CLOUD OF WITNESSES, LET US LAY ASIDE EVERY WEIGHT, AND THE SIN WHICH SO EASILY ENSNARES US, AND LET US RUN WITH ENDURANCE THE RACE THAT IS SET BEFORE US."
>
> HEBREWS 12:1

It is entirely within the realm of possibility that God takes men and women of faith out of time and then places them back into time at key points in history to bear witness to what He is doing. The Greek word translated as "witness" literally means "eyewitness." The writer of Hebrews describes these people as a "cloud" of eyewitnesses. Clouds form out of thin air, don't they?

Could it be possible that God would allow a deceased loved one to watch when an offspring wins a race that he always wanted to win, or could a mother who passed away be allowed to witness the daughter's graduation, or could God pull us out of time and place us somewhere in the past or future to be an eyewitness to something He is doing? Would He use a dream, a vision, to do this? Is this what happened with the prophets of old? What would qualify you for such an experience? According to the Bible, we would need to fall somewhere between Abraham the father of Israel and Rahab the prostitute.

While we may not solve all of these mysteries about time, we can understand enough to know that we need to think about time in every decision we make. After all, time is only a mystery to us. God sees the past, present and future all at once. Therefore, nothing catches Him by surprise. That means God not only knows the future, He knows our future.

This is why it is illogical not to put our faith and trust in Him to lead us. He has already been where we have yet to go. Faith in God isn't really a risk. The greater risk is to try to live a life without Him in it.

GOD NOT ONLY KNOWS THE FUTURE, HE KNOWS OUR FUTURE.

God created you for a purpose. He wants to see that purpose through. You have a destiny and a purpose. God could have put you anywhere on the earth at any time in history, but He chose now. Why? Because there is something you were created to do that can be done best right now right where you are. It is something only you can do. It involves lives that only you can touch, hearts that only you can reach. You have that much value to God.

If the days when you are on the earth are getting spiritually darker, that means you are part of God's plan to counter that darkness with light. He has saved the best of every bloodline to live right now. That means you.

It's time to arise and shine! You were created for such a time as this. You won't fail, because the God who gave His only Son to redeem you now waits to see what you will do for the Kingdom. Move forward! Keep going! It is a fact that God has already seen the road ahead and He has cleared the way for you.

Reflections and Meditations

Do you regret something so deeply that it seems to haunt you?

In light of this study of time, how does God view your past? How could you change your view of it?

How do you know that you can trust God with your life?

What would help you to pray in faith for God to forgive your past mistakes and guide your future?

If God is watching your past and future play out at the very moment you pray, and if the all-knowing, ever-present God who created you is with you right now, then what things will you begin to pray for today?

CHAPTER 3

THE MYSTERY OF CHOICE

On the road of life, we will remember a handful of decisions we make. We will remember where we were and who was with us. We might remember one as a difficult decision, or we might remember how peaceful we felt after making another one. We might look back and wonder what life might have been like if we would have chosen differently.

When we ask someone how they landed where they are today, they'll usually point to a handful of big decisions—the college they chose, their marriage, a job they took or turned down, what city they chose to live in. They'll look back at those decisions and say, "That's how I got here." They may even tell us those decisions shaped who they are as a person today.

What if I told you that every big decision that person ever made in life was the result of a thousand smaller, seemingly insignificant choices, choices the person could probably never remember that contained a "DNA" which eventually led to those major decisions?

These thousands of choices are what have put us where we are today—me writing a book, you reading a book. Those seemingly small choices have actually made us who we are today.

The answer we are after is to the real mystery of choice—the cause. What causes us to choose one way or another? Can we change the outcome of our major choices by paying more attention to the minor ones? Can we change the DNA of our decision-making? To do that, we'll need to look at one of the most powerful forces on earth, and you probably weren't even aware of it until now.

SEEMINGLY SMALL CHOICES HAVE ACTUALLY MADE US WHO WE ARE TODAY.

"We make our choices, and then our choices make us." We often hear such a saying, and it is generally true. We can inherit personality traits from our parents, and we are given spiritual gifts from God, but our character is the true gauge of who we are. Our character is built as the byproduct of the choices we make.

Even what seem like small choices make a direct impact on how our lives turn out. A choice we made five years ago can limit the decisions we have available today. The effect is on the smallest of decisions.

For example, imagine a man in his twenties named Will who anticipates a big raise at work. He decides this would be a good time to get out of that old car and get into a brand-new one. Then Will convinces himself that the base model won't do. He'll soon be able to afford it, so why not go all out with the loaded model? To pull it off, Will has to go with a slightly higher interest rate and slightly higher payments, but what will that matter when the raise comes in? The raise is just a formality. There's just one signature standing between Will and the keys to his new car. This is the moment of choice.

Of course, we know by the setup to this story where it goes. Will doesn't get the raise. In fact, out of his frustration and stress, he pushes the wrong buttons with his boss and ends up getting fired. Two months later his brand-new car gets repossessed.

Now, five years later, things are going much better. Will has learned from his financing mistake. He has even learned to live within his means. In fact, he has some money in savings for the first time in his life. He meets a wonderful woman and gets married. Now it's time to buy their first home. One problem: Will's credit is affected by one rash decision he made five years earlier. In fact, Will is paying more to rent the home he is in than the home he wanted to buy, but Will is stuck, and so are his wife and the child they are expecting.

Small, or at least what seem like small decisions can play a significant role in the direction our lives take. That's why we need the wisdom of God embedded into our decision-making process.

Allow me to give some personal illustrations about decision-making. For one thing, I've found that I make much better decisions after spending a significant time in the Word of God each morning. I have more peace and less confusion. I don't always know what important decisions I'm going to face that day, but reading the Word prepares me for when they come. When I miss my Bible reading, I notice the difference in the decisions I make.

I also place a high value on maintaining an atmosphere of peace around me. I'm willing to sacrifice in other areas in order to keep peace in my life. For example, most people plan to get to an airport one hour before their plane leaves. I travel a lot, and have learned that I do not want to sacrifice my peace for that kind of a schedule. Instead, I set my schedule to be at the airport at least ninety minutes, and usually two hours, before my flight leaves.

To me, rushing to make a flight adds stress to life. Life has enough of its own stressful situations without me adding another one to it. Stress creates a filter that hinders our decision-making.

Another reason I leave for the airport so early is that I recognize there are dark forces that don't want me to get where I'm going, and another is the simple fact that, whether dark forces or not, it is easy to be delayed by a half hour or more. It happens all the time. I would rather wait an hour in the terminal in peace than to arrive just as the plane starts boarding. There are two things I've learned are not good at an airport—excitement and surprises. It is always better to be bored at the airport.

Those two little habits in decision-making—reading my Bible every morning and getting to an airport early—both serve to help me make better decisions. They do even more than that.

For one, reading my Bible in the morning creates an atmosphere of peace around my decision-making all day. It acts like insulation or a barrier to chaos and confusion.

For another, removing stress from my life allows creative thoughts to flow. Picture a "peace dome" of protection over the creative thoughts that would be lost, shoved out of the mind by rushing. Stress removes peace, and peace is worth protecting.

PEACE

The Hebrew word for peace, shalom, is more of a verb than a noun. The Hebrew understanding of shalom means to remove chaos and anarchy from around us. Peace is more than just the result of "not-peace." Peace is an action that we take.

Peace welcomes the Holy Spirit into our choices. We want the Holy Spirit involved in even the smallest decisions. This doesn't mean we stop in the middle of the road in our car, pray, and then wait to hear from God before we make a turn. We're not to be impractical or strive for the impossible. We simply involve the Holy Spirit in our lives and stay connected to the very Spirit of God. We invite the Holy Spirit into every decision we make by exercising our spiritual senses.

Decisions that become habits, a routine, mean we no longer have to think about them. They become second nature. We may make a wrong choice again. The goal is simply to make our greatest choice be in favor of a deeper relationship with God.

This relationship with the Holy Spirit carries over into areas of our lives where we may not even think about our choices. How we respond to our husband when he forgets to fill up the car and leaves us stuck on empty, or what we say to the cashier who accidentally rings up the gallon of milk twice. Our response is a choice. As the DNA of choice is developed, the choices become habits.

We can live a life that involves our spirits in every choice we make. We can do that without even having to think about it. This spiritual atmosphere, this life inside our "peace dome," becomes a part of who we are.

One my favorite sayings is, "Peace is the potting soil for revelation." It is the optimum growing condition for right choices.

Technically, a choice is a mental process whereby we judge the merits of two or more actions and then take one of those options. There are stages to every choice, but they all happen very fast. The whole process can happen in seconds.

PEACE IS THE POTTING SOIL FOR REVELATION.

Every choice begins with a stimulus. A stimulus is something that prompts a response. It starts the ball rolling. As soon as that happens, we come to an immediate and mysterious place called "the moment of choice."

The moment of choice happens right after the stimulus and right before our choice. That moment determines whether we respond out of the spirit or out of the soul. We're deciding if we'll say, "He hit me so I'm going to hit him back," or, "He hit me but Jesus said to turn the other cheek."

Between the stimulus and the moment of choice is a filter. This filter is something we have developed over time. The moment of choice comes from the stimulus, through that filter. The filter is determined by whether we are led by our spirit or our soul. In that nanosecond of time, that "Moment of Choice," everything noteworthy in our lives is established. That seems unfair, doesn't it?

The Apostle Paul was talking about the "Moment of Choice" when he wrote that the things he wanted to do he didn't do, and the things he didn't want to do he did.

Our problem is that after the choice is made, it's too late.

What we need is for that moment of choice to get stretched out, to seem longer.

Again, every choice starts with the stimulus. A stimulus is something that prompts a response. The phone rings, our spouse asks a question, the traffic light turns yellow, the cashier gives us back too much change, or someone backs out of a parking space right into our brand-new car.

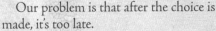

Right after the stimulus comes the split-second decision called the "Moment of Choice." This moment is where most of our decisions take place. These aren't the big choices like which house we're going to buy. These are the hundreds of choices we make every day. These tiny choices make up the

DNA of our character. To make the moment of choice even harder, it has complex layers we'll just call "filters."

Filters are thoughts that become a lens, or filter, to how we perceive the world. Our filters play a major role in the choices we make every day. The filters determine whether we make choices from the Tree of Knowledge, which is the soul, or the Tree of Life, which is the spirit. The longer we have these opinions, the thicker our filter becomes, the darker the lens through which we view the world around us. The darker our lens becomes, the less likely we'll have a spiritual response.

The filter determines if we get out of our car to hit the guy who just ran into our new car, or if we stop and realize that had it not been for the grace of God we would have backed into a car just last week.

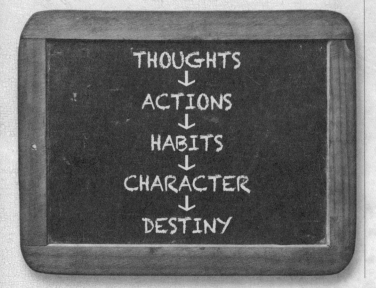

THOUGHTS
↓
ACTIONS
↓
HABITS
↓
CHARACTER
↓
DESTINY

Inside the DNA of every life-altering decision, we find the strands of a thousand smaller choices. Those choices became a pattern, that pattern became a reality, and that reality became very difficult to escape. It's almost as if, in making a choice, we no longer have a choice.

How does a thought or an opinion about something lead to a life-altering decision? Our thoughts become an action, our actions become a habit, our habits form our character, and our character determines our destiny.

FOR I DO NOT DO THE GOOD I WANT TO DO, BUT THE EVIL I DO NOT WANT TO DO—THIS I KEEP ON DOING.

ROMANS 7:19 NIV

We cannot change our destiny without going all the way back to the beginning and changing our thoughts.

It is never too late to start our future history by changing the DNA of our choices at the root. This comes by changing the way we think.

This is a very personal process that occurs in the deepest parts of our minds and spirits, so I am compelled to write from my own personal experiences. As I do, I am painfully aware of the many ways in which my personal character was developed. In fact, I'm reminded of an embarrassing time that I argued with God about a tiny piece of paper.

Many years ago, I was walking down a hallway and felt the Spirit of God impress me to pick up a little scrap of paper off the floor. I thought, "Lord, they have people who get paid to vacuum and sweep this floor. I don't even work here. I'm just visiting a friend."

Again, I felt the Lord tug at my heart to do this seemingly minor and trivial task. The words, "Son, pick up

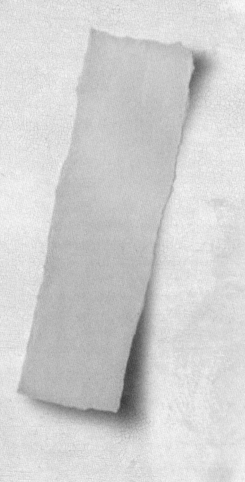

the paper," nagged at me. Again, I didn't understand how this could be such a big deal to God, so I struggled. Finally, because I wanted to be obedient, I went back to where I had seen the paper, bent over and picked it up.

End of story. Literally, that is the end of the story. You may have expected more, and certainly I thought I would find some reason for picking it up, but nothing else happened. No one saw me pick up that paper. The paper itself had no significance, no secret message on it of any kind. I deposited the paper into the nearest trash bin. Nothing changed at all—not at first, anyway.

The stimulus was the piece of paper, out of place, on the floor. The moment I saw it, I had a choice. I knew the paper wasn't supposed to be there. My choice was whether I was going to keep on walking, or bend down and pick it up. During that moment of choice, my soul and my spirit were in a battle. My soul was the voice in my head that said, "That's someone else's job," but my spirit was telling me to pick it up. I had to decide at that moment whether to follow the soul or the spirit.

That paper became the first of many choices God began to provide when I had to decide if I would do what He impressed on my heart to do, or if I would do what my head told me to do. Most times, it was a decision on the most unimportant things. From that point on, it was as if God put me on a test course.

Over time, I began to understand that God was using these mundane acts to drive me toward something even bigger than obedience. God was working on that mysterious space of time called the moment of choice.

These moments of choice, many of which seem insignificant, confront us all day, every day. Small choices reveal our filters, our thought processes that predispose us to make a decision out of our soul or out of our spirit.

Remember that our soul is made up of our mind, will and emotions. Our spirit is made up of wisdom, communion and conscience. Filters don't just show up one day. We don't just wake up one day and become an axe murderer because someone bumps into us on the sidewalk.

Filters develop over time and become part of our decision-making apparatus. If our filter says, "That's not my job," it will show up in other areas of life, sometimes at the worst possible time. We may act on that filter at home when we should be sharing chores around the house, or with our children when we should be helping them with homework, or helping fill the printer with copy paper when it's easier to leave the job for someone else.

As we practice our small decision-making, we can clean the filters that have been clogged, that keep us from making choices that honor God. Whereas we once may have said, "That's not my job," we can adopt an attitude that Christ adopted on the Cross when He said, in essence, "I will make the sins of the entire world my job, my responsibility."

Recently, I was pouring a drink in our office lunchroom and spilled the entire container on the floor. The team was pushing a very busy schedule in the office, as well as juggling my travel schedule. The ministry staff was hungry for every minute that I could spend with them. When the spill occurred, my filter had been so programmed by those years of God telling me to "pick up the paper" that I instinctively reached for the tools to clean it. Just as instinctively, the staff tried to push me toward my next meeting and promised they would clean it up.

However, my training in taking care of the mundane things of life was so strong, my moment of choice served to overrule the team, and I helped clean the spill. If anyone on the team had ever felt they were too important to clean a mess, they would have received a life lesson that day that no employment manual could have taught as clearly.

I'm not saying this would be the best choice every time. It may not serve a purpose for an Army general in the middle of a war, or if I were speaking at a banquet where a waiter dropped something. The point is, in even the smallest choices we make every day, we can choose to follow what our spirit says and learn to overrule what our soul says. When we do, living by the spirit becomes a habit that will serve us well and may even be an example for others.

In the same way that we learn decision-making by clearing our mental filters of soulish thoughts we also hear from God—not by trying to turn up the voice of the Spirit. We have to learn to turn down the voice of the soul. We turn down the voice of the soul by removing the filters that build up, we turn down the voice of the soul by creating habits that establish an atmosphere of peace through prayer and the Word so that we can hear the Spirit, and then we start to develop spiritual filters that help us make better decisions.

> ## THE ART OF HEARING GOD
> Not trying to turn up the voice of the Spirit.
>
> Learning to turn down the voice of the soul.

Behind every big decision we have ever made, we can find a trail of small, seemingly insignificant choices, choices led by our souls or led by our spirits. God created us this way. He knows how important the small choices are. He knows that the small choices lead to actions that become habits, those habits form our characters, and our characters determine our destiny.

God has sent you the help you need. He sent His very Spirit to comfort and counsel you, to guide you along the way. The Holy Spirit is a gentle counselor, though. His whisper can be drowned out by the opinions and desires of your soul. God created you with a soul that will serve you well when it is in submission to your spirit. The soul learns submission through simple acts of obedience. Your soul is an excellent servant, but a cruel master. Lean toward the Spirit. Listen for His whisper.

Reflections and Meditations

Have you ever experienced a "Moment of Choice" that turned into a disaster?

Can you retrace your steps to figure out what led to the last major decision you made?

Have you ever had an internal "nudge" to do something out of the ordinary that you didn't do?

Have you ever had an inkling to do something unusual that you did do? What was the result?

After reading this, what do you understand about how choices determine destiny?

What could you start doing today to make better decisions in the future?

CHAPTER 4

THE MYSTERY OF THE LAW OF ATTRACTION

God has built a force into the fabric of Creation that can be called the "Law of Attraction." Ever since God set it in motion, the Law of Attraction has been a great and important principle. It worked long before the New Age movement gutted the meaning and turned it into something that it is not. Run an Internet search on the Law of Attraction, and it will turn up dozens of New Age books and teachings. Most will explain how we draw positive energy to ourselves by sending out positive energy.

The results, according to these authors, can be both health and happiness. That's too bad. Had these New Age thinkers taken the time to look at the Bible, they would have seen how this law really works. It is much more powerful, and more complex, than they ever imagined it to be. It is also much more obvious.

We can see the Law of Attraction working all the way from the laws given to Moses to the teachings of Jesus. It is included throughout the wisdom teachings of King Solomon in Proverbs. God built the Law of Attraction into the very fabric of Creation.

The basic Law of Attraction in the earth states that a negative charge will attract a positive charge. The earth could not be held together without it. It is essential to the table, chairs, ground and sky all around us.

God works in our lives according to this same law that upholds the world. The basic Law of Attraction for us states that when we allow ourselves to decrease, God is justified in giving us an increase. Let's look at that more fully. But first, let's be clear that the New Agers got it wrong.

THE BASIC LAW OF ATTRACTION FOR US STATES THAT WHEN WE ALLOW OURSELVES TO DECREASE, GOD IS JUSTIFIED IN GIVING US AN INCREASE.

The Law of Attraction is not something that can be manipulated or controlled, though many have tried. It's a law that can be understood only within the context of the principles and character of the God who created it. It is a mystery.

Today's popular view of the Law of Attraction is a counterfeit and different than the biblical Law of Attraction. New Agers believe that the Law of Attraction is about asking "The Universe" to give or bring back to you what you project. For example, they believe that when you give out positive thoughts or energy it will attract positive energy or actions.

The real Law of Attraction is not about what the universe gives or takes away. It's about the way the "operating system" of the Kingdom of Heaven was set up by God. This system was created before sin ever entered into the heart of man. It is a strange system where the way to be exalted is to be humble. The way to become truly alive is to "die" to self. The way to receive is to give. At the core of this seemingly backward Kingdom, what holds it together is a gravitational field called faith, and not just any faith—faith in God.

The best way to describe the Law of Attraction is to start by looking at an atom. All things that we know to exist are made up of atoms. In the world of the atom, a negative will always attract a positive. That's how all matter is held together. It is called an atomic bond. An electromagnetic force draws and holds atoms together based upon the attraction of a negative charge to a positive charge.

Let's leave the subatomic properties of this law to the scientists. What we're interested in is uncovering how this law applies to our lives. We all want to live lives that attract blessings. Even those in the New Age are trying to do that, albeit through the wrong means. What we don't want to do is try to manipulate this law for our own personal gain. That's why the Bible says God loves a "cheerful giver" (2 Corinthians 9:7). Scripture speaks not just to the act of giving, but to the heart behind it.

Negatives attract positives. What I mean by negative is that whenever we give, we create a negative charge. That negative charge then attracts a positive charge. When we give to the poor, it subtracts something from us. That subtraction leaves us with a negative charge that attracts something positive toward us.

When dealing with this law, we must be clear to differentiate between God's true Law of Attraction and the version the New Age has stolen and counterfeited. Think of holding an envelope. If I'm a New Ager, and I think that inside this envelope is a dollar bill, then I will put energy into "The Universe" through my thoughts, which will return to me more envelopes with more dollar bills. But if I think this envelope holds a debt to be paid, then by my thoughts

I will put energy into "The Universe" that will attract more envelopes filled with debts and accounts to be paid.

Let's look instead at how the Bible describes the Law of Attraction. Long before we had microscopes that could see inside molecules and cells, God was articulating the Law of Attraction in His Word. The Kingdom of Heaven is built upon an invisible foundation of seemingly illogical, opposite things. The way up is down. The way to receive is to give. The way to be comforted is to grieve. The way to be strong is to be meek.

It makes us understand why Jesus spoke in parables. The Kingdom of Heaven is constructed like nothing else. It is put together like a riddle, but a riddle isn't a riddle if it doesn't contain a clue, and the Bible is full of them.

Bible principles don't always make sense without applying the Law of Attraction to them, which simply states that a negative attracts a positive. The negative charge we talk about in the biblical Law of Attraction is not a value statement. It does not mean that one charge is bad and one is good.

Think of a magnet and its unseen force. We can't see how the magnet pulls metal toward it. We just know that every time we get a magnet near some metal, they attract. The magnet uses a natural law of physics.

Spiritual laws can be just as predictable and measurable as physics. When a negative charge is put out, a positive charge is attracted.

A negative charge when it comes to the Law of Attraction or science isn't a bad thing. It is a good and needed force. So what creates a negative in the spiritual realm? For one thing, giving.

Giving requires the right attitude. We give from our heart, without expecting anything in return from the person we give to. That sacrificial act, losing something, subtracting something, creates a negative charge in the spiritual atmosphere. That negative charge then attracts a positive response from God, a blessing. That's how the subatomic world works. That's how the Kingdom of Heaven works. It's not, however, how the world works. In the world, "the squeaky wheel gets the grease."

Jesus taught us differently. When it comes to giving, He didn't teach us to give in order to get. Whenever we give, whether it be money or goods or services, even time, we do it with no strings attached. Think about it. If there's a string attached to our giving, we didn't really give. It may have left us physically, but it never left us emotionally because we expect it to return to us when we ask.

It is equally true that when we give we set in motion a reaction so that God gives back to us, but if we give for that purpose alone, we fail in our giving. This is why the Bible tells us not to even let our left hand know what our right hand is doing. We just give. We let God work out how we will be rewarded.

What about fasting? How does fasting create a negative charge? Fasting is denying our flesh and soul. In the same way, we create a negative charge in every area of our lives as we sow into the spirit instead of the flesh.

Fasting increases our spiritual sensitivity. In a sense, we are "starving" our flesh and feeding our spirit. What happens if we tell everyone we're fasting? We lose that negative charge. We get our reward by people patting us on the back and saying we're doing a good job fasting. That puts us right back at neutral. Whoever we tell might think we're real spiritual because we fast, but that's nothing compared to the positive that God wants to bring to us in the spirit realm.

The Law of Attraction is also shown in the verse of Scripture, "Let us continually offer the sacrifice of praise to God, that is, the fruit of our lips, giving thanks to His name" (Hebrews 13:15). How can praise be a sacrifice? Because when we spend our time to praise God, especially when we don't feel like it, we create a negative charge. The result is the positive, that God inhabits, lives, dwells in those praises (Psalm 22:3).

Prayer also creates a negative. We sacrifice our time and our tears to come to God for the sake of unsaved relatives and neighbors, for the sake of our families and the needs of others. This is why we don't pray only for God to bless us and give us things we want. If we pray only for our own needs to be met, we don't create a negative that can attract a positive.

In the story of Job, he lost all his wealth and even his family, then his friends tried to convince him it was his own fault. He suffered in every way, but finally received his breakthrough when he started to pray for his friends.

Reading God's Word creates a negative charge because we are giving our time to spiritual pursuits instead of personal gain. Many times, God's response to that negative is an immediate positive—revelation! We read His Word and He gives us revelation about an issue we're dealing with, or He opens up a spiritual truth that we never saw in scripture. Reading God's Word will always attract a blessing, unless our motive is to bring ourselves glory through the revelation we receive. All revelation from God is to bring glory to God.

"Negative" Spiritual Charges
Giving
Fasting
Praising God
Praying for others
Reading God's Word

These have been pretty obvious. Spiritual disciplines are. What else is there to uncover about this mystery of the Law of Attraction? The Law of Attraction will often look similar to the Law of Sowing and Reaping. These two laws work hand in hand.

We see the subtlety of applying the Law of Attraction in one of the most famous sermons Jesus ever gave. The "Sermon on the Mount" found in the fifth chapter of Matthew is one of the places in Scripture where the Law of Attraction is spelled out for us.

Matthew 5:2-12

2 Then He opened His mouth and taught them, saying:

3 "Blessed are the poor in spirit, for theirs is the kingdom of heaven.

Humility is the negative charge that attracts promotion and spiritual advancement from God.

4 "Blessed are those who mourn, for they shall be comforted.

Compassion for others is the negative that attracts the positive of comfort and peace from God.

5 "Blessed are the meek, for they shall inherit the earth.

The negative charge of self-control and non-self-promotion attracts the positive response from God of an inheritance from the King.

6 "Blessed are those who hunger and thirst for righteousness, for they shall be filled.

The negative charge created by desiring after the spirit and not the flesh attracts the positive charge of true fulfillment.

7 "Blessed are the merciful, for they shall obtain mercy.

The negative charge that comes out of treating others with mercy attracts the positive of God's mercy.

8 "Blessed are the pure in heart, for they shall see God.

The negative charge created when you don't defile your spirit with the fleshly, carnal desires of life opens your spirit to see the pure, supernatural glory of God.

9 "Blessed are the peacemakers, for they shall be called sons of God.

The negative charge created when you create peace in an area where there isn't any invites the positive response from God as a King to His heir.

10 "Blessed are those who are persecuted for righteousness' sake, for theirs is the kingdom of heaven.

The negative charge created when you endure ridicule while following God attracts the positive response of favor and authority in the Kingdom you defend.

11 "Blessed are you when they revile and persecute you, and say all kinds of evil against you falsely for My sake.

12 Rejoice and be exceedingly glad, for great is your reward in heaven, for so they persecuted the prophets who were before you.

One of the greatest negatives you can ever create is that of being martyred for your faith. Enduring hardships, ridicule and false accusations and still standing strong in your faith attracts the positive attention of Heaven here on earth and in the life to come.

The Sermon on the Mount shows how the Kingdom of Heaven works. It is basic cause and effect. We see it throughout the Bible.

The Law of Attraction works in all areas of life. We enact this law by fasting, praying, blessing others with our words, and honoring others even when they don't honor us. We want to live a lifestyle that attracts the positive attention of Heaven. To do that, we have to sow to the spirit and not to the flesh. Creating a negative charge is really just sowing the visible into the invisible and trusting God to take notice.

THE DREAMER IS AT WORK IN HIS OFFICE AND HEARS A COMMOTION DOWN THE HALLWAY.

He gets up to see what's going on. He sees a lot of his coworkers standing around in a circle but he can't see what he is looking at. They were making lots of noises. Some people were screaming and others were laughing. Finally, the dreamer pushed through the crowd and saw what everyone was looking at. It was an alligator that one of the women workers had brought, and she was letting it walk around the office. The dreamer couldn't believe no one was saying anything about an alligator loose in the office. He asked the lady who brought it where she got it, which later seemed like an odd question. The dreamer later wondered why he didn't ask why the alligator was at work, and why it was on the loose. He didn't remember where she said she got it, but he told her if she needed a place to keep it, she could keep it in the dreamer's office. Then the dream ended.

God is so incredibly gracious that He gives us dreams sometimes to show us actions that are dangerous to us and that need to change. This is called a "correction dream." On the surface, it seems innocent enough, but remember that dreams are symbolic. This is one of those rare dreams when you can identify one key symbol and almost interpret the whole dream.

The metaphoric meaning of animals in dreams is often connected to certain characteristics they carry. Horses will generally represent power. Dogs, though, are known as "man's best friend." When we see a dog in a dream, it will usually represent a friend. Any cat owner knows that whereas we choose a dog as a pet, a cat chooses us as an owner. Cats are aloof and independent. Therefore, in a dream, a cat will often represent an independent spirit.

Earlier in this series of books, we saw a dream with an alligator that was in a brood of snakes. Because of the snakes, we knew it represented something more dangerous than a snake. In general, when we look at an alligator, what is the first thing we notice? Its big mouth. Alligators have a big mouth. They also have a very powerful tail. So an alligator represents a big mouth with a powerful tail, which can be spelled T-A-L-E. What does that sound like? Yes, alligators or crocodiles in a dream frequently represent gossip. Without even interpreting the rest of the details in this dream, with an office worker turning an alligator loose in the office, we pretty much have the complete meaning.

The dreamer has experienced gossip in the workplace. At first he wanted it to stop and considered having it removed. But as he stuck around, he ended up enjoying it. In fact, by the end of the dream, he invited the gossip's owner to come by his office. This dream illustrates the old adage, "If you don't have anything good to say, don't say anything at all." Its counterpart states, "If you don't have anything nice to say, come sit down next to me." Another fitting one is, "Anyone who will gossip to you will gossip about you."

WHEN WE LIVE A LIFE RULED BY OUR SOUL, WE ATTRACT THOSE WITH "LIKE" FRUIT.

We don't want the spiritual attention that hanging around with a gossip brings. Some people say that if someone starts to gossip, we should just walk away. I teach people to take it one step further and tell the gossip, "I can't listen to you talk about that person, because if it were me you were talking about, I would be devastated. I'm sure you would be, too."

Walking away from a gossip takes willpower. Correcting a gossip creates a negative charge that will attract blessings from Heaven! ∎

There is one area where the Law of Attraction seems to work in reverse, and that is in regards to relationships. Ungodly people seem to attract those who walk in darkness. Godly people seem to attract those who walk in light, the exception being those who are seeking to turn from darkness to light.

We know the sayings "birds of a feather flock together" and "misery loves company," but could there be more to those sayings than meets the eye? Is this one of the reasons the Apostle Paul writes that we are to set our mind, our thoughts, on things above and not on things of this earth? Could it be that by living a life of saying "no" to the Tree of the Knowledge of Good and Evil that we attract those who eat from the Tree of Life as we do? This truth seems to be summed up by Solomon when he penned, "Evil pursues sinners, but to the righteous, good shall be repaid." (Proverbs 13:21)

The bigger point is this: When we live a life ruled by our soul, we attract those with "like" fruit. When we live a life ruled by our spirit, we attract the blessings of Heaven. This attitude of heart can also attract the people who would be most willing to help us reach our God-given purpose, and we can become the person to help others reach the purpose for which they were created. That is God's divine intent for the Law of Attraction.

Built into the structure of every substance on earth is this mysterious force, the Law of Attraction. We can attract others to us based upon our thoughts and actions. We also attract the blessings of Heaven or the curses of this world based upon what we choose to focus on and place our faith in.

The passage in Galatians 6:8 of sowing and reaping is not just about the words we speak or even actions we might take, it is about the friends we make as well. It is another example of the biblical principle of the Law of Attraction. "For he who sows to his flesh will of the flesh reap corruption, but he who sows to the Spirit will of the Spirit reap everlasting life." What we focus on we will sow into. Thus, if we sow ungodly actions, we will attract ungodly people who have the same actions.

The great news is we have a powerful "reset button." We have the ability to stop the attraction of darkness. It starts with repentance, which requires we say no to the world and change our focus back to God. That change in spiritual perspective goes even deeper that actions alone—we have to change the way we think. The Bible tells us what to think or focus on.

"Whatever things are true, whatever things are noble, whatever things are just, whatever things are pure, whatever things are lovely, whatever things are of good report, if there is any virtue and if there is anything praiseworthy—meditate on these things."

Philippians 4:8]

The moment we change the focus of our thoughts, the atmosphere around us will change. Darkness leaves and we allow Heaven to draw near. This is how we were designed to live. This is the will of God for our lives. We are blessed and called to become a walking blessing to others. All of this is set in motion by the mystery of the Law of Attraction.

Here is one last way to create a "negative" that will attract the positive of the blessings of Heaven: Be a river.

Remember that Jesus described the Holy Spirit as a river of living water that flows out from us. When we stay in tune with the Holy Spirit, the lives of people around us can be changed, too. We will attract people to us by the very Spirit of God, people who will help us fulfill the purpose for which we were created. Those are the same people we can help to reach the purpose for which they were created. This is God's purpose for the Law of Attraction.

The Bible says a river flows out from the throne of God. Not a lake, not a pond—a river. One key to attracting the continued blessings of God is to recognize that holding onto what we have will hold up what God wants to give us. When we let the river of God flow through our life by allowing the Holy Spirit to use us to be a witness of God's existence to others, we will see more of His presence active in our lives.

BE A RIVER.

Reflections and Meditations

When you do something nice for someone else, do you expect something nice to happen to you?

Think of a time when something nice did happen to you. Did you do anything to make that happen?

What kind of "negative" have you ever created that could attract a "positive" from Heaven? Giving?

Praising God? Praying?

How can you fulfill the scripture not to "let your left hand know what your right hand is doing"?

What can you do today to create a negative that will attract the positive?

CLASS IS IN SESSION!
with John Paul Jackson's Online Classroom

Take one or all four university-caliber courses written by John Paul Jackson. It's never been easier to take a quantum leap forward in your spiritual walk. Each of these 23-hour courses can be streamed right from your computer, tablet or smartphone. Learn in-depth:

The Art of Hearing God
Understanding Dreams and Visions
Prayer and Spiritual Warfare
Living the Spiritual Life

Begin your journey to understand all God has for you by going to StreamsMinistries.com. Click on "Online Classroom."

Get all these great resources from Streams Ministries!

ABOUT THE AUTHOR

John Paul Jackson is recognized as a minister who reveals God, awakens dreams, and leads people to Christ and closer to God. For over 30 groundbreaking years, he has been known as an authority on biblical dream interpretation.

He renews passion in people of various faiths and age groups with his sincere explanations of the unexplainable mysteries of life, and enables people to relate to God and others in fresh and meaningful ways.

As an inspirational author, international speaker, insightful teacher of true spirituality, television guest, and host of his own television program, *Dreams and Mysteries*, John Paul has enlightened thousands of people across the world. He finds satisfaction in his role as a youth mentor, advisor to church and national leaders, and the promotion of the spiritual arts.

@JohnPaulJackson
Facebook.com/JPJFanPage
StreamsMinistries.com